The Illusion Warrior

The Illusion Warrior

Musings of Mind and Spirit

J. MICHAELS

RESOURCE *Publications* · Eugene, Oregon

THE ILLUSION WARRIOR
Musings of Mind and Spirit

Resource Publications
An Imprint of Wipf and Stock Publishers
199 W. 8th Ave., Suite 3
Eugene, OR 97401

www.wipfandstock.com

ISBN 13: 978-1-60899-535-6

Manufactured in the U.S.A.

Dedicated to all those fortunate souls
who have discovered *A Course in Miracles*
and all who will someday

Contents

Preface xi

A Miracle With a Sense of Humor 1
Most Profound 2
Jesus Had a Bald Spot 3
Fly Me Home 4
Chosen I 5
The Curtain 6
World of Fools 7
A Most Unusual Change of Heart 8
The Paradox of the Pain 9
The Same Land 10
He Promised Me Miracles 11
A Decisive Way 12
Holy Schedule 13
Tender Accusations 14
Big Nose 15
Poet of a Different Ilk 16
The Next Intangible 17
The Abundant Norm 18
Extraordinary Work 19
Never More Sane 20
Give Me a Million 21
The Grandest of Themes 22
Happy Tunes 23
Sacred Cows 24
Thy Three 25
See 26
Lost in Amusement 27
Better Stuff 28
Simply Blessed 29
End It With a Sigh 30

In Love Again 31

Better Views 32

Better Plans 33

Writing in the Dark 34

Sins That Have Never Been 35

Indistinguishable 36

Moving Faster 37

Lovely Mind 38

I'm Home 39

The Poet's Fill 40

Starting to Remember 41

Dubious Whereabouts 42

Greybeards Unite #2 43

Getting Gushy 44

Derivatives of Love 45

Holy Stuff 46

Faulty Frame 47

Tending the Form 48

Not a Very Good Poet 49

God's Blanket 50

All That Passes My Eye 51

Clothing My Brother 52

I Close My Eyes 53

One Set of Footprints 54

A Little Fun With Fred 55

Namaste 56

Love Pills 57

A Somewhat Joke 58

Words Only Matter 59

One Total Son 60

Room to Stay 61

Shadow of a Doubt 62

The Overnight Poet 63

Family Whole 64

Something We All Have Planned 65

Returning the Prodigal Son 67

Exactly What I Do 68

Love Sublime 69

Six Pixels of Love 70

Given and Received 71
Lonely Tear 72
An Overnight Sensation 73
The Best Possible Thing 74
One Fine Relationship 75
Apple of My Eye 76
A Most Trusted of Themes 77
The Greatest of Plans 78
To This My Words Attest 79
A Global Conversation 80
Only You 81
Miracles Indeed 82
Silly Void 83
All I Seek 84
Bye and Bye 85
Conversing as Sober 86
Competition as a Surly Art 87
Spare Me the Details 88
Good Friends 89
Stepping in Crap 90
Spoken in Similar Ways 91
My Wife and I 92
Best Friends 93
The Poems 94
Virginal Key 95
Simple Grail 96
Details 97
A Call to Witness 98
One Once More 99
Why Am I Smiling 100
Hey Sash 101
Similar Form 102
What's a Poet to Do 103
Becoming Christ 104
Choose Wisely 105
Setting Up a Joke 106
Born, Live, Die 107
Image Collage 108
Such a Pity 109
Bit Head 110

Preface

THE ILLUSION WARRIOR STEPS forth, devoid of weapons and armed only with truth. He knows that what he sees is false. It must be. It certainly is not the work of a loving Creator or even a rational one. He struggles with the vastly popular opinion to the contrary but is embraced by the overwhelming and awe-inspiring certainty of truth. He knows, and he knows that he knows. It is one of those things that require no justification or validation from an external source. The warrior has lived too many years that were failed by the seeming validation of a world endorsed by its scientists, its protagonists, and its suitors. He has lived too often in the world of uncertainty, fear, and betrayal. He has seen too much that denies truth, belies reason, and lies profusely to itself and its constituents. He seeks to tear down the illusory walls that separate him from his brothers and sisters, his holy kin that has accepted so little. He rips back the heavy curtain that obscures the ever-present light that exposes the lie; the deceit that has for so long denied his holy family the reunion they so richly deserve.

His is a lonely journey, though he is daily joined by new warriors who have seen the invisible light and felt the Holy Presence just beyond the curtain; those brave few who dare defy the obvious and popular notions of reality. This, his new clan, join him now in his quest to revamp common thought, overturn the false obvious, and tear down the perceptual filters that have for so long blinded us all. The warrior is less lonely now that he feels his brothers and sisters by his side, all seeking for what must be a better way, a higher ground, and a certain and infallible truth. He takes comfort in their mutual need to be free, whole, and completed in a way not available in the world of illusion. He sets aside now the insufficient and temporal sex of the world of form, the excitement of the revolving pleasure dome, and the violence that denies his holiness. He moves toward a reality more deserving of the magnificent mind he has been graced with, towards an intelligence without bounds or pretense. He insists on love and grace and oneness. And he is willing to lay down the paltry life of form to have it. Yet he knows he loses nothing, for nothing is what he owns and everything is what he is owed by divine inheritance.

He bids you come along and join the newfound band of warriors who claim their divine rights and ever-blessing. He waits in loving anticipation for you to meet the long forgotten but never lost Master of the Universe. He smiles in expectation, knowing you are about to greet your destiny. And he rejoices in the knowledge of what you are about to see, know, and become.

A Miracle With a Sense of Humor

My friend, the J-man
Has posed some things quite well
He has issued some promising ideas
And provided some stories to tell
He is having a grand time, as am I
Playing with words and ideas
To open that closed third eye
Tis a passion and joy for me
I know He feels the same way
Tis joyful play, it is
We play the loving game
And within that love is a giggle
And that giggle is divinely sent
I'm dealing with a paradox
A miracle with a humorous sense

Most Profound

I need to pause for a bit
After that last one
I'm still pulling my socks back on
And returning the hair to my head
I'm still spinning around
Amazed by what just happened
It seems most profound

Jesus Had a Bald Spot

It's been rumored that Jesus had a pot gut
A bit of a bald spot too
It's told he dressed in plaid, no less
Shoes that needed a shine or two
He may have had a lisp or stutter
Perhaps a case of A.D.D.
I don't think it matters to Him
He knows it doesn't matter to me
For what we love and cherish
Is the soul and mind of the man
It's time we denied the obvious
It's time we all understand
That form is really quite worthless
A dried leaf upon the wind
It has little or nothing to do with
The man or the soul within

Fly Me Home

Fly me to the moon
But please don't stop there
My final destination awaits
It is but a one way fare
Take me much farther
I will gladly pay my way
Fly me to the sun
On this fine chosen day
I yearn for the Source of All
I yearn for the judgment day

Chosen I

I've become more simple
I chase, no more, the day
I've chosen to wait it out
To be shown the better way

I decline sophistication
False dignity rejected too
Simple truth and love
Is now my righteous due

It feels so much lighter
The complex and difficult die
No strain, no push or pull
The simple me is the chosen I

The Curtain

Forgiveness dissolves the curtain
That hangs between you and I
A curtain of dense illusion
It is but an empty lie

When I forgive you my sins
That curtain shall fall away
To reveal the Son of God
Standing on both sides this day

We shall see each other finally
For the truth of who we are
Blind eyes will be opened
Giving vision that sees quite far

Way beyond this planet
Or the world that hides us well
Seeing all the way to Heaven
As far as I can tell

World of Fools

The dream's shallow offerings
Beg us to accept far less
Than the blessings meant for the Son
Blessings that dreams contest

The difference is quite pronounced
The quality far apart
The one disguised as pleasure
The others are from the heart

The shallow payments are meant to hide
Our consent to be unholy
Our willingness to blindly abide
The pain and suffering it provides

The Father's Blessings are far more attuned
To our soul and mind's direction
To leave this world of fools

A Most Unusual Change of Heart

The Paradox of the Pain

These pains are burdens I carry
From sea to shining sea
In one eye, I see Christ
In the other, pain is what I see

I don't want Heaven *and* hell
I want only my Father this day
Why can't I leave this pain
Leaving only peace to stay

The Same Land

Do you see this, my brother
Does it enter your heart
Have your eyes popped open
Are we having a good start

If you truly see this
Then raise your knowing right hand
I will take your gentle word for it
We've arrived both in the same land

He Promised Me Miracles

He promised me miracles
And here they are
Brilliant poems written by layman
No one can stretch that far

If you want to see miracles baby
Then listen up right here
These little gems all qualify
As balm to all we fear

He chose an old man
Who had lived life askew
Filled him with hope, he did
And now tells me what to do
He said, *Become a miracle worker, my son*
Get out there and share them
You'll know just what to do

So I zipped up my heart
So none would fall away
Til I get to my destination
Giving up miracles, of which I obey
They are the promise He made

A Decisive Way

Did I throw you with that *change of heart* thing
Do you still ask yourself why
Has it confused or bemoaned you
Or still does it attract the eye

My change of heart was simply
To write no poem at there
You may enter your change of heart
Let it attend but your care

For it doesn't really matter
Either of us can say
That which has changed our hearts
May put us in a decisive way

Holy Schedule

I abide thy schedule, Dear One
I wait gently upon Thy Knee
Waiting for the Hand of my Father
To be bestowed upon me

Your Will is my will, Father
I need nothing You do not provide
All is known to me anywho
There is nothing or nowhere to hide

So I will be most patient
Now that I know the chosen way
Let me know when you get a minute
Pencil me in someday

Tender Accusations

Accuse me not, of sedition
I but challenge the ordinary way
Who in their right mind would want it
Any other way

If my words accuse you
Know that I meant them well
Notes intended to guide you
To Heaven and away from hell

Big Nose

I have a big nose
And a bit of thin hair
My wrinkles stare back at me
Yet show me I am but fair
For the light and love within me
I'm obligated to let out
It might come from benediction
Or from my big old snout

Poet of a Different Ilk

Words come differently to me
Ignorant of construction
Whole sentences appear to agree
On poem or prose released
The meter is unconscious
The rhythm a mystery too
The rhyme that soon emerges
Amazes and astounds me true
I guess I'm a poet of a different ilk
Denying the ordinary its due

The Next Intangible

Tangible packaging for the intangible
A form for the formless
A thing derived from no-thing
It's quite a tidy little mess
Yet I relish the thought of it
Writing it thrills me too
I can't wait for the next intangible
To work its way on through

The Abundant Norm

You're feeling your oats, my Friend
I'll try to keep up with You
As long as I humanly can
We've never had quite so much activity
As blessed with this autumn morn
I'm amazed at your dexterity
In providing the abundant norm
With such things to inspire it
To challenge, and leave, its form

Extraordinary Work

Gimme a high five bzillion
We've done some extraordinary things
I must give You the credit
I never knew what love could bring

I'm quite honored You chose me
To deliver these sane, sweet words
I would give You heart and soul
To blend with equal worth

I am You, You are me
This extraordinary work we've done
Has called and set me free

Never More Sane

I've never felt more sane in my life
Past years filled of ordinary insanity
The things the world calls life

We are offered far sweeter things
Like making our hearts come alive
Treasure beyond imagination
Belying the puny in our lives

I choose this route of innocence
I renounce the worldly way
I have found my loving Savior
By His side, I will pray
Safe and sane and eternal
Waiting for you, for the same

Give Me a Million

This is why I want the mil
I'll have no need of worry
Of debts and costs and bills

I want never to betray them
These gems that come my way
Never to be confused with dollars
So far beyond that, they stay

So give me a free ride, if you will
I will spend it wisely so
Using it only for good things
To maintain the poet's flow

The Grandest of Themes

You are my audience
Of a small and settled few
Getting past the barriers
That tried to hinder you

You first must like poetry
Then the spiritual you agree
Works with *The Course*
Turning all three

If you make it past these fair filters
I believe you will agree
We are an audience quite small
Who study the grandest of themes

Happy Tunes

I'm hearing the Allman Brothers
Kicking out killer sweet licks
Banging down the rhythm
That makes it all go *click*
All those friendly notes and chords
Playing those *Statesborough Blues*
Bringing all of it together
To give me some happy news
(Happy news from the blues, who knew?)

Sacred Cows

A sister and friend once said
You like to wrangle the herd
She said You love those sacred cows
The most she's ever heard

Neither of us know when
Either of us don't know why
But it sure seems You're riding high

Riding the range
Roping the herd in line
We both would like to learn how
You ride herd over said bovines

Thy Three

Thy Will is my will, Father
Thy Plan is my plan, O Captain
Thy Truth is my truth, my Brother

See

See Jesus in plaid
See Him in your neighbor
See how others are clad
Notice Him in fat sister
See Him with toupee askew
See Him in your brother
See Him in you

Lost in Amusement

Fully throttled for amusement
Geared up to get involved
With a wide variety of distractions
I think I like them all

There's so many to choose from
So many that catch my eye
I wish I had a few more hands
To keep them all alive

What to do next, my main concern
This button or that, the choice
Mind bubbles arrayed geometrically
I hope to give them fair voice

So many want to speak to me
They strive, my attention to get
It's all getting me hopelessly lost
Mega amusement's not such a big hit

Better Stuff

It goes straight to my heart
I start to crumble
Days and nights gone by
Start to well up in my eyes

Sins past committed
Now brought to bear as pain
Knowing they were but errors
That caused our sullied strain

In the center of our being
In the core of our soul
The world hopes to beat us
But we're made of better stuff, I'm told

Simply Blessed

I am a fraud
No matter whom I profess to be
Not who I say I am
It could be two or three

Call me not poet
Nor writer claim to be
No more illiterate labels
No matter what we see

I am but one thing
That I am blessed to be
Composite and devoid of them all
Simply blessed, is all I be

End It With a Sigh

What is it in us
That lures us back to sleep
What makes the temptation so
What puts it in full view of us
And makes our slumber grow

Awakened is our natural state
Truth in full light exposed
Time to open our eyes
Time to put sleep behind us
And end it with a sigh

In Love Again

Go out, my little lovelies
Amuse and amaze
Kick up some dust in the process
Maybe start a new craze

Touch a heart here, a mind over there
They are intended for eternity
Yet they need start somewhere

So perhaps they land in your lap
Perchance to haunt your mind
Maybe to cause a listen
Or offer an answer to find

Accept them as my children
I give them to you, my friend
My goal is to bring them all
To show us love again

Better Views

I pay homage to the quill
Tis more than ink and steel
It is the point of contact
Between the world and what is real
The carrier of happy thoughts
The bearer of Godly News
The river flowing from there to here
The bringer of better views

Better Plans

I sense judgment in the air
No known location
Yet I know it is there
Unable to detect an origin
But I feel its icy stare

Affirm the loss of it
Know it by its feel
Let it not board at home
Know it to be not real

Deny its steely glance
Leave it and let it go
We have better plans to advance

Writing in the Dark

I write in the dark
The words carry their own light
They illuminate my page
And unlit regions of mind
Gentle blessings, they are
Diamonds for all to find
They are my blessed offspring
I love them with all my might
They carry me to the light

Sins That Have Never Been

Trouble has arrived
To mine the troubled me
Side trip taken down lonely road
Slippery slide through memories

So many mistakes
That don't mean a thing
Stir and dump my regret
All over everything

Tis difficult to see a loved one
Stumble and fall and demean
The beautiful essence within them
That which is pure and clean

I had a hand in it, I did
Disappointed my little sister
Caused her pain and grief
My soul wants to forgive it
And reclaim a little relief

Yet my Father smiles knowingly
Saying I never sinned
He knows what is within me
All sins that have never been

Indistinguishable

Long have I held back
Relying on the distant abstract
Jesus was far too personal
Thought I might get side-tracked

So keep him at bay, I did
Denied him his due
He presented me brotherhood
His heart offered too

Now I give him mine in return
No longer do I bar the way
He is my brother and teacher
I would have it no other way
One in love and mind
Indistinguishable we stay

Moving Faster

Everything is moving faster
Time has speeded up
Communication is getting closer
We must be headed up

The world is controlled by ego
Like it, a false concoction made
But truth is of our Father
Unlike the world, it will never fade

My heart laughs with joy
As I see the tide start to turn
Love will soon sweep over us
Saving us from the churn

Lovely Mind

The body begs indifference
To all but itself
Needing all in the way of attention
Leaving your soul upon the shelf

All truth is denied there
All cause truly misplaced
Seeking to deny our power
Wanting to slow its pace

For it needs misdirection to live
A lie it provides instead
It denies the mind a place
To lay its lovely head

I'm Home

It is oneness, my friend, it is oneness
It is oneness and it's so damn beautiful

I start to glimpse the future
Having forgotten the past
Coming attractions are the moment
In which I now take repast
The place where I end my fast

Home, at last, I am Home
Never let me leave this moment
Never again to roam

The Poet's Fill

These are big pages
I'm sure you've noticed by now
Lots of room left over
It seems a pity somehow

What do you think we should do
Any ideas for using it
I think it leaves room for you

So go ahead and do it
Write all over me, if you will
I'd like you to get your money's worth
And finish the poet's fill

Starting to Remember

I'm starting to remember
The Source from whence I came
The beginnings of my ego
Are lost beyond its frame
It is God I am touching
It is the Face of The Divine
Starting to sense my origin
My Home, I soon will find

Dubious Whereabouts

There may be some dubious whereabouts
Possibly ranging from near to far
I'm not sure I can hang my hat on it
Til I see what shields the heart

Once my direction is found and set
I'll question the world no more
I'll simply take one last look at it
And leave it forevermore

Greybeards Unite #2

Greybeards unite, all of you
Let's show them what oldies can do
I'll do my part, you do yours
This is what I will do

If you grow grey with me
I know you have wisdom to share
Reach deep within sister/brother
And bring out what you dare

The world starves for a bit of wisdom
A way shown back to grace
Better views of simpler places
That lights the wiser face

Come with me, gentle elders
Step forth, don't fade away
Bring with me simple fortunes
There is no better way

Leave not our younger brothers
Essentially, we are the same
Young and old together
All the same tigers to tame

Getting Gushy

I seek to erase some boundaries
That lie between me and you
So I'll write these lines til I effectuate
Perhaps touching a life or two

If it happens just once, I'll celebrate
A life lived well and forthright
If it happens but twice, I'll jump for joy
At the blessings bestowed that night
If it occurs beyond that, don't tell me
I may get all gushy and pee

Derivatives of Love

All those things we feel
All that makes for joy
We call them by numerous names
They are but derivatives of love
God is love, my friend
There is no more
Call it by any name you want
It is but Him we adore

Holy Stuff

Whole, eternal, and free
What else could we possibly be
We are made of holy stuff
All that our Father bequeathed

We are perfect, my friend
We are brothers joyfully bound
Each to the other in oneness
Our souls forever found

We need only see each other in truth
To know the Heavenly way
We need only to awake to our Father
To know that we are this way

So live no more in poverty
Claim the riches that are ours
Count no more what is missing
Claim only Christ's pure power

For yes, we are quite powerful
We are made of holy stuff
We are born again indestructible
God's gift is quite enough

Faulty Frame

The imperfect channel
This I appear to be
I would buy it myself
Except I've learned to see
Beyond the form that portrays me
To the truth of who I AM
Imperfect the form may be
But I am not its sham
I belong to a view much better
I subscribe to a higher way
Tolerate, please, the imperfect
Let it not get in your way
Listen, my brother, to the message
Ignore the way it came
Appreciate the gift it is
Never mind the faulty frame

Tending the Form

Tending to the form
Becomes an onerous task
Doctors and dentists trying to conform
Wearing a singular mask

Athletes and warriors
All trying on different forms
Bathing, clothing, resting away
Brushing, tanning, feeling okay
Healing, fixing, delaying old age
Nipping and tucking here and there
Freezing our face so no one will stare

Trying to preserve something that is not
Real or enduring, such a sad lot
Focus our time on the authentic goal
Less time on the body
And more on the soul

Not a Very Good Poet

I'm not a very good poet
I seldom know what to say
If it weren't for the Muse
I'd really need to pray
For of myself, I am nothing
Frail words can never convey
The Part of which I am something
That tells me what to say
Not that unlikely really
It's always what I prayed

God's Blanket

By its nature, it must be shared
This love, this oneness, this all
Unable to contain or want to
This love we must recall

It drives us beyond the pleasures
And the traps the world does set
It is our irrefutable companion
Despite any minor regret

It is that which binds us
One to another, single in heart
It is the blanket of God
To warm us by His Hearth

All That Passes My Eye

I write of Godly things and silly things
I write of baseball and baloney
Alongside the Christ and crowd
My poems have farted and belched
They have told tales to ponder alone
Or funnies to laugh out loud
They have spoken of darling babies
And brothers one and all
Christ explored with shoes forlorn
Soldiers bleeding as they fall
Angels sailing the skies
I write of damn near everything
That passes before my eye

Clothing My Brother

My brother is clothed only
In the projection I send fore
Behind that mask of illusion
The Christ light shines forth
Without the thoughts forlornly spent
My brother would surely be
Only what is Heaven sent

I Close My Eyes

My eyes are closed
Yet I am still here
The body fades in darkness
The mind and spirit appear

So when we leave this body
It will but yield to light
And show only truth as left
Death is but the ego's delight

We think without the body
We know without the form
Truth depends on nothing
Live is devoid of the storm

Peace is its companion
When lived within the light
No body may thus contain us
Eternity is our right

One Set of Footprints

One set of footprints
Painted through the snow
Heading off into oneness
What is it he knows
The steps stop in the middle
Nowhere else do they go
Those are my footprints
I made them through the snow
I stand here unafraid
Unknowing, yet at peace
Waiting for our Father to claim me
And absorb me in His Grace

A Little Fun With Fred

I slap you upside your head, Fred
I'll punch you in the gut
Might knee you in the balls
If it'll get you off your butt

For I love you too much
To let you stay and rot
When so very much awaits us
And offers an infinite lot

So kick it in gear, my friend
Awake and arise from trance
Kick up some dust if you want to
And ask your brother to dance

We will throw the largest party
Ever to be known to man
Everyone will surely be there
Everyone will understand

That anything is worth the doing
Only if it makes us one
Do what it takes to get there
It might be a little fun

Namaste

Namaste this day
It's the perfect thing to say
We honor each other, my brother
The *Namaste* way

Love Pills

Love pills in my bottle
Encased in joyous fold
Message sent from Paradise
All was prior told

Open your heart, my brother
Let the little pill in
Warm your heart, rest your soul
It's quite a way to begin

To stretch and extend ourselves
Attaching beginning to end
Becoming a complete and holy sphere
The pill expands from within

A Somewhat Joke

God will take me despite my language
It doesn't mean a thing
He loves me unconditionally
To Him my soul does sing

I've said some things quite crude
I have disavowed the norm
All just meant for salvation
All to obviate the form

Lessons come wrapped in assorted ways
Not always what we expect
To open our hearts and minds
To welcome what few respect

Don't be put off by the coarseness
Just another tool we use
To rattle the long held cage we're in
A somewhat joke by the Muse

Words Only Matter

I'll bet you're tempted to judge me
When I state things so crude
A holy man would never do such things
It must be considered quite rude

For we all know that Jesus never swore
It was way beneath His way
He had no need for crudeness
He lived a different day

Kindly remember, my friends
Words are just a way
To get inside your head for a bit
And beg listen to what I say
For the words, as such, only matter
When they comprise that of which we pray

One Total Son

The impulse to defy our isolation
Arises as we shed our separate ways
The coming together of dear minds
As we approach the holiest of days

The thirst for communication
Is subdued by ego's din
The noise imposed upon the mind
Distorts what comes from within

Yet we struggle to be clear
We yearn to become as one
May Christ take us beyond the noise
To speak as one total Son

Room to Stay

These are gifts delivered gently
No noise will they make at your door
Placed simply in front of you
To see it they attract you more

They will appeal, or not
I know not their destined way
Where they lodge, I know not
I pray you give them room to stay

Shadow of a Doubt

Wouldn't it be nice to know
Never forgetting nowhere to go
No guessing, no conniving, no show
One Mind getting it all
Less confusion, no answer to grow
So tiny and alone we need not be
One Grand Mind is ours to know
Nothing to speculate or debate
Knowing everything, zero left out
Confident we know each other
Beyond any shadow of a doubt

The Overnight Poet

I am the overnight poet
The one who jumped the fence
I have no need of answer
I need mount no pooh defense
One day, a middling geek
The next, paper receives my heart
I have had a bit of a peek
It's a lovely poetic start

Family Whole

I am called *papa*
The sweetest word I know
The sound approaches gently
Destined for my soul
From sweet baby to shining girl
Her light has lit my life
She has made us family whole

Something We All Have Planned

The sixty year poet from Flint
Here by surprise, no warning sent
An unlikely path to get here
It must have been Heaven sent

Small, frail boy to start with
Soon an athlete to be
Played all the way to adulthood
It happened too fast to see

Went through the *get it while I can* thing
Propped up his penis to be
The instrument of his achievement
Popping kids, all three

Got smart and went to college
Educated by profs and pot
Turned into career and profit
Turned out to not be a lot

The love that accompanied my travels
Surfaced to set me free
Beloved family born thrice
Two oldies, one youngie, we three

Healing the older man
Giving him his timely due
Now he's turned poet
No one seems to know what to do

We'll figure it out, my loves
We'll put in some time or two
God has put us together
And asked me to do what I do

Scorn me not for arrogance
I have not that deadly sin
Deride me not for confusion
I would never let it in
Praise me not as Jesus
I am just a simple man
Condemn me not as Satan
Until you understand
That to be a Son of God
Is something we all have planned

Returning the Prodigal Son

Come naked to me, don't be shy
Laying aside all clothing
That covertly hides our eyes
Let only truth confront us
Let bodies fade away
Let nothing come between us
Allow only love to stay
We are born again of each other
We are destined to be one
Returning to the Source of everything
Returning the prodigal son

Exactly What I Do

I'll take the job, I need no pay
I will consider it my honor
To serve You in this way
The blessings bestow me first
Before I give them away
It is a noble profession
To guide my pen this day

I make modest money
Little of material recompense
Yet the benefits are quite startling
Turning chaos into perfect sense

So deny me salary or vacation due
Please allow me to keep doing
Exactly what I do

Love Sublime

If I died whilst reading a poem
Right in the midst of fair words
It would be a most righteous death
Hopefully, you're not disturbed
For to be in the midst of love
At any given time
Is but to live in the moment
And receive the gift sublime

Six Pixels of Love

I bought your book, dear brother
I've started to explore your mind
You speak much of oneness
You know, the business kind

I praise what you offer on paper
I view it as gift of Mind
Long have I searched for oneness
You know, the holy kind

Given and Received

To give is to receive, it is true
No platitude nor cliché it be
Once the gift comes through you
You'll know what it is I see

No need to protect our interests
They are one in the same, you see
Love can only be shared
Given and received as free

Lonely Tear

I issue the call to come Home
A simple, loving message sent
Not a complex, intellectualizing moment
A heart's devotion is all that is meant

The love we have within us
Is more powerful than any known here
More potent than any philosophy
It exceeds the knowledge sphere

We have only to accept love's power
To know we are Heaven sent
Only to love our brother
To repair the mind long bent

It is quite simple really
The convoluted belongs only here
It is love and mind and power
That dries the lonely tear

An Overnight Sensation

A restless night became me
Pushed me to the edge
Offered a better way
I went to sleep a businessman
Woke up in the poet's fray

At 3:33am in the morn
Normal dreams left the building
Made way for the woeful yarn
Nicobod and Icobod appeared
And started a brand new game
Soon left the world of business
To paint in the poet's frame

An overnight sensation, I'm not
Perhaps only a few will see
The miracle worked on me that night
To render the poet I be

The Best Possible Thing

I know of no anticipated turns
The future is still quite vague
What lies beyond the very next step
Eludes and befuddles my brain
Yet fear never taints my footsteps
Nor deafens my refrain
Unknown and yet uncertain
Of what will heal my pain
I need no warranty of paper
It will be the best possible thing

One Fine Relationship

I feel most excellently guided
My knees don't knock or tremble
I hold account now with my Savior
The relationship remains quite nimble
We consult the Holy Spirit
Ask that He look our way
The next move is exquisitely planned
To not get in the way
Of footsteps destined for Paradise
Or hamper the Holy Way

Apple of My Eye

I'm sixty years old and counting
I'm headed for the door
I'd like to stick around and share
The world can always use some more

We had better talk fast, you and I
Not sure when the journey ends
Not certain I'll be able to come by

Let us cherish this time together
Let us help each other to fly
Let us be our one True Self
And the apple of my eye

A Most Trusted of Themes

I trust those in whose hands my life resides
I know to be trustworthy and free
The finest of companions deemed possible
The One and Only, the Holy Three
Fear never had a chance
Nor opportunity to disagree
This fairest of Fathers smiles and agrees
To the most wonderful of pacts
Your eyes will ever see
Unable to be lost, destined to be free
Assumed by a wondrous Whole
Captivated by beauty extreme
Love completely surrounds the event
And assures a most trusted of themes

The Greatest of Plans

A multilayered illusion
Can be quite difficult to see
Just when you think you've got it
Another layer is revealed to be

Direction need not be our concern
As long as truth remains our friend
We need not pursue a plan
We require no one to be
A guardian of our diplomats
A hired gun without a fee

Keep love as part of your heart
Let truth be your main man
Peace will soon accompany you
According to the greatest of plans

To This My Words Attest

I ask you to muse with me
Consider all things spiritual
On this we may all agree
No need to merge our bodies
No need to even see
We but meet in mind and spirit
The only meeting that we need

If these small writings
May impress upon your soul
The need to come together
Then I have achieved my goal

I ask nothing more
I pose nothing less
I simply want my brother
To open up and confess
To the lie we have all been living
Since situated in this mess

We are divine and eternal
We need no middling rest
We need but to come together
To this, my words attest

A Global Conversation

It's a global conversation
As fine as ephemeral dust
Though difficult it may be
Tis deeded to the human trust
A conversation for one and all
It's quite the conference call
It's a confab on the grandest of scales
A forum for universal tales
We soon shall see, how little we see
When we speak the language our minds do tell

Only You

Speak to me, Father
If it be You or Yours
Let no other voice intrude me
Let no other sound be heard

My ears are for You only
My eyes but see Your Face
Love is welcomed between us
To grace this holy space

I relinquish all other affiliations
I dispose of antiquated thought
Seeking only You, Dear Father
Finding that so very long sought

Miracles Indeed

Not everyone will recognize them
For the things they truly are
These golden delicious memories
In distant time seen far
The miracles clothed in time
For all the blind to see
Stripped of ingenious barricades
They release their shining star
Unveiled for all to see
They are miracles indeed

Silly Void

A conversation but had the following meaning
We spoke it in my dream
The mind is meant for finer things
Or so the story seems

I've been holed up here too often
I've taken a number of shots
Some fired at and by me
All formed a meager lot

It's time I silence my adversary
The one who drove me here
The one speaking of separation
The one of little good cheer

The time allotted has been wasted
Except for the lonely few
Except for those lovely lessons
That have shown me what to do

I will leave this intellectual wasteland
This barren plane of spirit devoid
To rejoin the Greater Mind
And depart this silly void

All I Seek

Oneness is all I seek
Love and truth is all I need know
Peace and joy are my partners
Nowhere but Heaven to go
Nothing else means anything
Except it may shelter love
I have no need of anything
When everything is what I love

Bye and Bye

Over and under, up or down
This seems my presented methodation
I never know who's coming to town

It might be silly me
Possibly the one seldom seen
Maybe a good or bad guy
Perhaps the juvenile scene

I have hopes for only the most holy
For the one with head held high
I seek to claim my Christhood
Leave the others, bye and bye

Conversing as Sober

It's like skating on thin ice
That covers the swollen stream
Which hides the unfiltered bias
When we make the enemy our dream

It but strands on decrepit bridging
Overlooking the depths within
Staring straight into the face of ego
Starting to stir up the sins

Beseeching a far lesser mind
To attend as who we are
Not bringing our A-game, or better
We lead our soul afar

So tame it, it's time
Deny entry to the family door
Let us meet up undivided
Conversing, as sober, the more

Competition as a Surly Art

Competition is a surly art
Stirring up conflict unengendered
Hoping to win the hearts
Of those from whom it seeks approval
Those who deal out the parts
For the roles we play oft determine
That which will rent our hearts
The need to prove better than another
May drive us to the devil's door
It may greedily consume us
Lest we prove we are but more
Than the guy who stands beside us
The one who will open the door
To the room where salvation awaits
And competition is donned no more

Spare Me the Details

I will deny you the details
They are a superfluous lot
Only the direction need matter
The rest is extraneous thought

For we serve a higher Master
We distribute but His fair light
The details are taken care of
No reason to fend, no reason to fight

For the trust bestowed upon us
Is what we owe in return
We need not know all the stops
On the train from here to where
To know our destination
And Who can take us there

Good Friends

We are quite good friends, for sure
Brothers in spirit, and more
We hold a certain confidentiality
That precludes an odious lore

We are on familiar terms
He lets me call him J
It is the way we relate
It makes for enjoyable fate

We love and like each other
We are equals in every way
Yet I defer to his intelligence
He has come the wiser way

We hold communion, with more invited
We share the Infinite Heart
We are but brothers united
Searching each other's parts

So if we laugh a bit loudly
Let it not diminish your view
For he and I are still Christ
And so, my friend, are you

Stepping in Crap

I've learned a lot these past few days
Stuff that truly matters
Having disguised myself for awhile
Leaving my soul in tatters
I have stepped in shit more often
Than I care to recall to mind
I have fouled up or out repeatedly
Only to finally find
That the things that bear repeating
Are those we trade in kind
To purchase our divine opportunity
And leave this crap behind

Spoken in Similar Ways

A wise man once told me
That words were invented to lie
To bypass truth self evident
And wrap it is deceitful plies

I do not doubt my erring brother
I know of what he speaks
Yet I know he has missed the point
Of that which truth does tweak

For our Beloved Holy Father
May do as He pleases to do
Even presenting dangerous phrases
To let His Love come through

So you see, even the vilest of intentions
May be set aside on any given day
And words may be used in love
Uttered to our God as we pray
And spoken to our brothers in similar ways

My Wife and I

My wife and I are beyond *sorry*
We have come to know each other well
We know the intent of the other's heart
We know where the other's soul dwells

So we simply let it go these days
We know it's not worth a pass
These silly things that try to snag us
And bite us in the ass

So we'll settle for simple love
We'll embrace it with all our might
Pleased to be with each other
With only Heaven in sight

Best Friends

I'm best friends with someone I can't see
Someone not within earshot
But that can hardly be
For he is so close to me
That it leaves no room to be
Apart, or even distant
When we are one, we three
He and you and me

The Poems

The poems have prompted me to be expansive
They have opened up my soul
No longer the tragic recluse
Stepping forth from the shadows as whole
Forgiving the incomplete its shortfall
Forgetting to pay the toll
I need not bear any witness
I need no crutch to hold
My life has bloomed because of them
They have made my life quite whole

Virginal Key

I come from the pragmatic world
The one of so called common sense
The one where all is upside down
Always seeking recompense
A price extracted we dare not bear
A cost too high and hardly fair

We may stay as long as we'd like to
We may dally the long sweet day
Yet pain and fear will stalk us
Insisting on the devil's pay

Swipe it away, we will
Deny the lie its place
Lift our head to the spiritual
Let the sun shine upon our face

Welcome the smile from Heaven
The warm and sunny glow
Dissolving this false world forever
Covering it in holy snow
Pure and white and innocent
The key to our virginal soul

Simple Grail

The simple Grail will be
The only Grail we'll need
No need of pomp or flourish
Only one bears holy seed
Simplicity is the greatest beauty of all
Elegant and simple solutions
Will refuse to let us fall
The simple Grail is the Holy Heart
Of the One Who loves us all

Details

Thy Will is my will Father
All else is just details

A Call to Witness

I call you to witness
The transformation about to take place
Only my brother may witness
The light that will protrude my face
For I have accepted the offer
Made in times ancient fair
Realizing my Self again

One Once More

I don't want to replace your Christ
I just want to mirror your Christ
Knowing again, we are each other
Becoming the One once more
Let us see what is upon us
Let us know It forever more

Why Am I Smiling

May the smile never leave my face
I pray it stays forever
For the joy that is now upon me
Deserves a more fitting place
My Father, my Heart, has joined me
To the rest of our Holy Home
Worry has simply departed
Certainty remains in its place
That I made the right decision
May it show upon my face

Hey Sash

I'd like to tell you something, Sash
About how you came to be
Grandma and I implored our faith
And asked God to let you be
The only child between us
The one that made us three
Now we live as family
As it was meant to be

Similar Form

I haven't yet picked my nose
And I haven't yet said *fuck*
I thought to get them out of the way
And pursue some literary luck

These words and thoughts, are just that
They lay but upon the will
Let our intent be honorable
Regardless the *yuck* we feel

Look past such false layers
Do not be drawn apart
They but shield our innocence
And seek to keep our hearts

So put aside your indignation
Seek truth in any form
Be aware it could be looking
For you, in similar form

What's a Poet to Do

What's a poet to do
Coping with a friend like you
Rollicking and rolling uphill
Laughter, our guide to truth
Tis a glorious laughter
Tis joy, through and through
Spending good time with my Savior
Spending good time with you

Becoming Christ

I think I'll become the Christ ere you
I will do so in full view
I believe Christ will enjoin me
As we stand together, we two
So don't just watch, my brother
Take a hand, take a hold
We'll both become Christ together
We can watch it all unfold
Or so, at least, I've been told

Choose Wisely

I choose wisely
This, my elected path
My companions alongside me
Will speak to that effect
I find myself in fine company
No one you would expect to see
Yet they sure are real to me
It is Heaven's fair troops who attend me
Brothers, long lost and free
Holy companions thought separated
Seeing how lonely it can be
Yet re-finding this path, I see
Will let me rejoin the free

Setting Up a Joke

You sure know how to setup a joke
Your humorous sense is apparent
I don't think I've ever heard such stuff
Or know anyone who would dare it
I consider it a privilege and honor
To laugh with you, old friend
I look forward to more of the patter
And to play with you again

Born, Live, Die

Born, live, die
This is all we get
When we place our faith in ego
And on the world we bet

It seems a paltry sum
So far beneath our due
I wonder what God will offer
You say you have no clue

Yet I know, with our Mind, dear brother
The place where all is known
That you know of His Holy Offering
And all that It brings home

For love is offered instead
Of the meager sum we see
Love that is life eternal
And offers up that life to be

Trade one for the other, be smart
Settle for pretense no more
Give not your mind away
Settle not for your soul being poor

Accept the offer our Father bestows
Become what we are
As Heaven only knows

Image Collage

It's an image collage, nothing more
Mirages placed on collective matter
To show us what bears no truth
All to cover what is most true
All to obscure the only real
It is as disjointed as this world
As ill fit as a lost piece puzzle
Holding no value, no worth
Trade it, my friend, for another
A world eternal and true
A world that rhymes with you

Such a Pity

We take the world so seriously
Let me, if you will, challenge your way
Let us look upon its results
Let us appreciate what is paid
For the bottom line is death
And pain along the way
Uncertainty fuels the fire
That chars us in its flame
Such a pity, it is
That we choose this lonely way
When so very much awaits us
In love and its comely sway

Bit Head

I am the Google man
I search for what I need
A techno-geek for many years
Leading others to repeat
The lessons learned in cyberspace
The bits in byte-wed heap
Forming particles of illusion
Dreams for the technically inclined
Pretty puzzles for the intelligent
Bypassing thoughts divine
Paying more attention to widgets
Than the Heavenly pervasive Mind

www.ingramcontent.com/pod-product-compliance
Lightning Source LLC
Chambersburg PA
CBHW071839090426
42737CB00012B/2298